FOOD FOR THOUGHT

Elizabeth Hunter

MINERVA PRESS
LONDON
MONTREUX LOS ANGELES SYDNEY

FOOD FOR THOUGHT
Copyright © Elizabeth Hunter 1998

All Rights Reserved

No part of this book may be reproduced in any form,
by photocopying or by any electronic or mechanical means,
including information storage or retrieval systems,
without permission in writing from both the copyright
owner and the publisher of this book.

ISBN 1 86106 880 8

First Published 1998 by
MINERVA PRESS
195 Knightsbridge
London SW7 1RE

Printed in Great Britain for Minerva Press

FOOD FOR THOUGHT

Contents

Dedication	9
A Plea	10
Waiting for God	11
No Rest	12
I Am Yours	13
Peace	14
Help!	15
In the Still of the Morn	16
Morning Prayer	17
Listen and Heed	18
Stewardship	19
My Lord and God	20
Adoration Prayer	21
Praise	22
The Still Small Voice	23
We Praise You	24
Adoration	25

The War Within	26
Your Majesty	27
Comfort	28
Magnificent Dream	29
Sharing	30
Faith	31
God's Children	32
Where are You?	33
Universally	35
The Coming	36
Lowly Birth	37
Winter. Town and Country	38
Rejoice	39
My Friend	40
At Sunrise	41
Never Give Up	42
Slow But Sure	43
Redemption	44
Easter Week	45
Holy Child	46
Deep Thought	47
God With Us	48
Contentment	49
A Thought for Today	50

Love	51
Easter	52
God's Weather	53
Summer Calm	54
Inspiration	55
Hallelujah!	56
Me	57
Crucified Jesus	58
True Value	59
Prayer	60
October	61
Creation	62
The Storm	63
The Lord's Direction	64
Awakening	65
Close of Day	66
Work	67
Spring	68
Life	69
Solitude	70
The Garden of the Soul	71
Hope	72
Autumnal Leaves	73
Sleepless Night	74

Autumn Vista	75
Repentance	76
My Hope	77
Questions, Questions, Questions	78
A Different Story	80

Dedication

Clear my mind, Lord, that only thoughts of You may enter.
Clear my soul to allow only Your grace.
Clear my heart that it may always love You.
Cleanse my whole being till I meet You face to face.

My mind will focus on Your goodness,
My soul will no longer thirst,
My heart is full of Your love for me,
My whole being will put You first.

A Plea

Let me, Lord, enjoy the moment,
Not always striving for the next.
Let me look with awe and wonder
At all the works Thou didst create.
Not to fret o'er this life's trivia:
It will all fall into place,
But let me be both calm and humble,
Seeking for Your help and grace.
Let me be kind to other people
Not just caring for myself;
Grant I follow in Your footsteps,
Seek to do my Father's will.
Let me sometimes look around me
Finding what I can improve;
And then, O Lord, to seek Your mercy
For all the things I did not do.

Waiting for God

Have pity, Lord, now I am old,
And my mind lacks concentration.
My body now is feeble
And I feel strong frustration.
I still wish to serve You
But can no longer work.
I only know that You are here
And from me will not shirk.
I give my soul to You, Lord
And let me be resigned
To let others care for me,
To serve me and be kind.
And when You wish to call me
I'll be ready to come home
Looking for Your gentle hand
To guide me to Your throne.

No Rest

Dear Lord, I'm retired from the world of work,
Yet there are still not enough hours in my day!
But I'll never retire from my work for You
Which I gladly do without pay!

If I make someone happy who once was sad
And help anyone who is needy and poor
And do what I can for the homeless, too,
I need to come knocking on Your door.

For I want Your guidance and your help
To give me the courage and the hope
That I may keep healthy and of good cheer
With Your divine strength in me to cope.

And, Lord, when I retire from this, Thy work,
It will be when You call me home,
And I'll know that I can rest with You
And never need again to roam.

I Am Yours

Take my feet, Lord, and walk me in the right way;
Take my hands to work for You and always pray;
Take my eyes to see Your beauty all around;
Take my ears that I may hear Your every quiet sound;
Take my head, Lord, and help me understand;
Take my voice to spread Your word in every land.
Take my whole self, for I belong to You
And let me do whatever You want me to.

Peace

Lord, let there be peace in our hearts,
And peace in our families too,
Let us take peace to those we meet
In clubs, work places and the street.

Let peace abound in organisations,
So that peace in our country will rule
And give peace to every other nation,
So the world could have a second Creation.

But if there's one, with hatred and greed
This evil will rapidly spread around.
So let each of us always pray to You, Lord,
That we may live with one accord.

Give us peace, Thy Peace, on earth,
And goodwill to every land
So that as brother and sister we may live
And to each other Your peace to give.

Help!

In temptation, Lord, I turn to Thee,
For I'm in sore distress.
I'm but a weak and mortal soul
When put severely to the test.
I know that You will help me, Lord,
You know it's You I need.
It is so simply easy, Lord
To do just what I please.
I know it would displease You
But it's hard to turn away.
I ask Your Hand to guide me
So I will not sin this day.

In the Still of the Morn

In the still of the morn,
Before the dawn
You enter my heart –
Please do not depart
But guide my day
Along Your way
So good work is done
For everyone.
Each night You're there
Giving Your care
So I rest in peace.
You never cease
To watch over me
Wherever I be.
Please teach me to pray
Both by night and by day.

Morning Prayer

Good morning God, I'm here again.
You've seen me through the night.
Thank you for another day,
I want to serve You right.
May I always wear a smile
To brighten someone's day,
To show them, Lord, that I love life
Whether sorrowful or gay.
May I watch my tongue, oh Lord –
It tends to run away.
May I just say kindly things –
Keep hurtful words at bay.
Thank you for my talents, Lord,
They are gifts from You to me,
So let me not feel boastfully, Lord,
But meek and humble be.
And may this day be fruitful, Lord
In everything I do,
And may my hands be useful, Lord
In work and praise to You.

Listen and Heed

Thy voice speaks when we are still,
If we listen, we do Thy will.
For Thy grace we now would plead
To bless this day, and every deed
In work or play that we will do;
We'll do it all for love of You.
And every person that we meet
As brothers or sisters we should greet.
Love them as You taught so well
When on this earth You once did dwell;
Be there for them, today – tomorrow,
Listen to their joy and sorrow.
And when this earthly life is done
Our time of trial will be won,
We hope You'll open the heavenly door
To where we may live for evermore.

Stewardship

Everything, God, belongs to You,
What e'er we have or own.
It's only in our hands in trust,
To give account when we come home.
When we come before You
You'll ask us how we used
The Talents that You gave us,
Or have they been abused.
What we've done with surplus wealth;
Have we helped our poorer brethren
Or did we hoard it all away?
It can't be used in Heaven.
We cannot say we did not know –
You showed us when on earth
The way to live and share with all
Our goods, ourselves, our worth.
You will know the honest truth,
To You we cannot lie.
So may I, Lord, forget myself
And work for You until I die.

My Lord and God

I know that You are Three in One
With Jesus Christ Your only Son,
Who's with us each and everyone.
My Lord and God how great Thou art
That Thou shouldst come into my heart.

Your Holy Spirit was sent to earth
To help us all from time of birth
And guide our efforts to prove our worth.
My Lord and God how great Thou art
That Thou shouldst come into my heart.

I love You dearly every day
And try my hardest to obey,
So that from You I'll never stray.
My Lord and God how great Thou art
That Thou shouldst come into my heart.

And when life's span of trials are done
And life eternal has been won
Then may I live with Christ Your Son.
My Lord and God how great Thou art
That Thou shouldst come into my heart.

Adoration Prayer

O Holy bread of God,
You're present in the Host.
Here I kneel before You,
Father, Son and Holy Ghost.
I wait awhile in silence
Listening for Your voice
To tell me that You're always there,
But giving me a choice
To choose to go my way or Yours.
You give a just reward:
If I follow along Your path
And praise my God and Lord.
My soul and all my being
I offer up to You
In praise and adoration
With thanks for all You do.
So my God I listen
Waiting to hear You call,
Ready and willing to obey
And give to You my all.

Praise

Praise the Lord all my soul,
All that is in me praise His holy name.
Blessed is the Lord in His kingdom.
Great is the Holy One above;
He is mighty and has done great works.
He is powerful and forgiving.
All the wonders of the world
Are the works of the Creator,
The Omnipotent of the universe.
Praise Him for His goodness;
Praise Him for His greatness;
And praise Him for loving me.

The Still Small Voice

Oh, my God, I love You!
You're always by my side,
No matter what I do
You're always there to guide.
I try so hard to listen
To Your small silent voice,
But worldly thoughts distract me
And so I have no choice.
I ask for concentration
To help me without fear
To overcome distraction
And know that You will hear.
I ask You for Your blessing
On all I do this day,
I listen to Your quiet voice,
Hear every word You say.
I pray for people everywhere
That they may listen too,
Then peace will reign within their hearts
And all will turn to You.

We Praise You

We praise You for the seasons,
New life arrives in spring;
We praise You for the summer,
Long days and warmth You bring.
We praise Your autumn glory
With leaves of every hue;
We praise You for the winter,
Frost and snow the earth is due.
We praise You for all the months
In ever changing ways;
We praise You also for the weeks
That number all our days;
We offer praise for all the hours
When we give our time to You;
We praise You every moment
In everything we do.

Adoration

I worship and adore my God
As You watch from the heaven's above.
I honour and glorify You, my Lord
As You surround us with Your love.
I thank You for the use of earth
With all its colours so bright,
For all the peoples who make friends
And work with me for Your delight.
I thank You for Your loving care
And guidance every day,
I try to live a life of prayer
And carefully listen to what You say
And ask that one day we may share
Our life with You for aye.

The War Within

Oh, God, my soul is yearning
To feel Your loving peace.
To stop the turmoil in me
And let the raging cease.
Still my aching spirit
Which longs to sense You near.
Quiet me so I remember
With You I have no fear.
Come to me, oh Jesus,
I'll love You all I can,
I'll pray for You to guide me
As Your servant, which I am.
My best I'll do to please You,
Forget my woes and care
And listen to Your silent words,
Saying my burdens You will share.

Your Majesty

Oh Lord, You're in the mists of time,
Hidden in Your splendour.
To each and every one of us
You are loving, kind and tender.
We only have to call You
We know You're never out,
But calmly listen to our pleas –
We know You'll never shout.
We tell You all our problems,
Our woes and worries too.
We also thank You for our world,
And everything You do.
The angels round Your throne adore,
We join their hymns of praise
And some time in the future
Upon Your face we'll gaze.
We will then be glorified
And be with You always.

Comfort

Be still and know that I am God.
Let your soul be calm;
Take deep breaths of My pure air,
It's like a healing balm.
Think of all I have to give,
I'm generous with My gifts.
I give to each and everyone
The courage that uplifts,
The spirit and the will to work;
There's so much to be done
I need your heart and hands to aid
The Work I have begun.
So, my child, be not afraid,
Life is but a trial,
Just do your best to work with Me
For I'm with you all the while.

Magnificent Dream

Visit the sick and lonely,
Feed the poor of the land;
House and comfort the homeless,
Give ear and a helping hand.
If we all did this together
What a heaven on earth it would be.
No more sorrowful people
For such care would make us all free!
No more guilt to torment us,
No more heads in the sand –
Oh yes! What a magnificent dream –
And one that is wonderfully grand!

Sharing

For what I cannot have
Let me not be sad.
But for what I've got,
Let me be very glad.

What's the use of money
Unless I help the poor?
What's the use of treasure
Only kept in store?

But good deeds done on earth
Are much more use than gold;
And they build up a treasure
In Heaven, I am told.

So let me pray for wisdom
And share the gifts I hold,
And not to crave for riches
But be generous, kind and bold.

Faith

Lord, in the days you lived,
There were beggars in the street.
No homes had they;
No food to eat.

People passed them by
Without a care or thought.
They had homes and
Good food was bought.

Lord, we still have beggars in the street,
Homeless with no food.
Do we still just pass them by
According to our mood?

Or do we show them pity,
Drop a few coins in their path;
Stop and have a little word –
Have a little laugh?

'What You do to others,
You also do to me.'
This is what You said, Lord,
Help me this to see.

God's Children

Come to me, ye little children,
Whose souls are not yet stained,
Who have the innocence of your birth
And by the world have not yet been maimed.

May your mothers teach you prayers
So you can talk to me
And learn that I am in every sphere,
On land, in sky and sea.

When growing to maturity
Learn what's right and wrong;
Remember then what you've been taught
And grow up good and strong.

I allowed you to be born
And I'll guide you throughout life
If you'll remember to talk to me,
I'll help you in all strife.

And when I want to call you home
To live with me for ever
I'd like to say, 'Well done, my child,
For your constant life's endeavour.'

Where are You?

In storm and tempest, are you there?
Volcanoes, earthquakes – are you there?
In wars and famines – are you there?
We ask 'where?'

Look at people – how they care –
They forget themselves
Helping others in despair.
I am there.

Many give their time and money,
Many simply kneel and pray.
So don't you think it rather funny
That you wonder if I'm there?

I am there in all disaster;
I am there when things are good;
I am there for ever after –
I am there.

I am there to test my people.
I am there to make them think.
I am there to give them courage –
I am there.

I am there to love and guide them;
I am there to give them Grace.
I am there for I've redeemed them –
I am there in every place.

Universally

Every moment of the day
People of the world do pray.
From East to West
When not at rest
They adore in every way.
From dawn to dusk and back to dawn
Always somewhere a new morn.
And on Christmas day
We all say
Bless the day that Christ was born.
He came to earth to bring us hope
And show us all how we can cope
To fight for good
As we all should,
And all evil to revoke.

The Coming

Advent prepares for the coming
Of the Saviour's birth.
Everyone is scurrying
To celebrate on earth.
Jesus was born in a stable,
No comforts as we have today,
But everyone there was able
To kneel by the babe and pray.
Mary and Joseph adored Him;
The shepherds came at the call;
Three kings brought Him presents
And the beasts slept still in the stall.
We prepare now for His coming,
And rejoice in His birth once again
For had He not been born to save us
Sin on this earth would reign.

Lowly Birth

Jesus was born in squalor,
In a smelly cattle shed,
With no clean running water
And straw only for His bed.
Joseph must have worried
And Mary be very sad
That the only Son of God be born
In conditions so very bad.
But love abounded in that place
And Mary wrapped Him well
While the animals there provided warmth
In this story we love to tell.
Today He'd be taken into care
If born in such a state,
With germs and dirtiness everywhere –
What news it would create!
But Jesus came to show us
How humble we should be;
Not to seek possessions
But to find eternity.

Winter
Town and Country

The land is covered in a mantle of white,
Pure and crisp and clean and bright.
Bare trees are etched with a silvery hue,
A picture of beauty in our view.
Puffy clouds wear a pinky tinge
Surrounded by a hazy blue fringe.
A gentle wind sways the evergreen bower
Sending down a powdery shower.
The earth is still – not a soul about –
Just the birds darting in and out.

I sit alone in a cosy warm room
Yet my thoughts are filled with doom and gloom
When I think of the homeless on the street
With no warmth or food to eat.
My conscience stirs – but what can I do?
Except give alms and pray to You.
It seems so little when action is needed.
Remember, though – powerful prayer is heeded
Even above the town's mucky slush
And the continuous roar of life's long rush.

Rejoice

Jesus was born in a stable
To show us how humble to be,
Yet not only this did He come for
But to save us for eternity.

He died on the cross to redeem us
From our evil and sinful ways,
He showed us how to live our lives
And how to fill our days.

So when we greet the Christmas morn
And rejoice in the infant birth,
Remember He is our Saviour
And praise Him for all our worth.

Allelujah! Hosannas! Let us sing,
Glory to the Heavenly King!
Peace may there be upon this earth
And all our joy-bells ring!

My Friend

Close your eyes, my child;
Your thoughts they may run wild,
But ponder on My spirit –
Your mind will clear to hear it.
I'll whisper in your head
And say that I'm not dead.
I am Eternal life
And I'll help you in your strife.
You seek now for perfection
Following My direction.
Satan tempts you so
And you know you must say no.
So turn to Me in prayer
And your burden I will share.
If you trust in Me
I will ever be
Father, brother, friend
And give life without an end.

At Sunrise

How wonderful the sunrise
As it glows across the sky
With the pink of the heavenly clouds
Ascending way up high.
They drift towards the heavens
Like our prayers rise up in praise
And the messengers awaiting
Take them somewhere beyond our gaze.
The Lord will listen kindly
And decide if they are good
While we await His answer
And hope it's understood.

Never Give Up

'I want the Lord to take me,
I no longer wish to live.'
This is the cry of some folk
When they've nothing left to give.
But you have a lot to give, my friend,
With you we like to talk
And offer you a helping hand
And guide you when you walk.
We also need someone to help
As we try to do good deeds,
One day we'll all be sick or old,
Want help to tend our needs.
So calm your soul and rest in peace
Until your Maker calls for you
And we will try to understand
Your feelings with what you've been through.

Slow But Sure

I can no longer kneel to pray,
My joints are stiff and creak.
So I sit in a comfy seat
With cushions at my back and feet.
My mind is still alert and clear
So when I pray I have no fear,
For God will listen if I'm sincere.
Though I'm old and slow to move
I'm not idle or in a groove;
I knit and sew and read and talk –
I even go for a short walk.
I weed my garden with a long hand tool
And when I'm tired I sit on a stool.
I listen to music, quiet and calm,
It soothes my mind just like a balm.
I write long letters to my friends,
The work I do never really ends.
I live alone, yet I'm not alone,
For God is always in my home.
And when I'm down and feeling low,
I'm not for very long, you know.
I speak to Him and He comes near
To make me good and give me cheer.

Redemption

From the babe of Bethlehem grew a meek and holy child,
A placid boy who worked with Joseph undefiled.
He grew in stature strong and bold, waiting for the day
When He would roam around the land to teach us how to pray.
He showed and told us how to live so we might be redeemed,
But He was crucified and died – or so it seemed.
But on the dawn of Easter morn, He rose up from the tomb,
And proved to us He was God's son, and lifted all our gloom.

Easter Week

Holy Week has come again
For us to celebrate.
Maundy Thursday – food of life
Given to commemorate.
Good Friday on our sins we dwell
For these our Jesus died.
Saturday: empty and forlorn,
The Apostles tried to hide.
But Easter morn all gloom dispelled
With our God's approbation;
Christ had risen from the tomb
And proved to every nation
He was truly Son of God;
Our Master, Lord and King.
The Scriptures had then been fulfilled –
Hosannas; Allelujahs sing!

Holy Child

The most precious child ever born,
Came in Bethlehem one winter's morn.
His parents knew this special babe
Was born for us, the world to save.
The simple shepherds from angels heard
That there a glorious event occurred.
Three wise men from far and wide
Followed a bright star for their guide
To find this child in stable bare
Surrounded by an ethereal air.
Thus this day a Saviour came
To show us all how we can gain
The joy of Heaven for a prize
And see our God with our own eyes.

Deep Thought

A joy to give,
A joy to receive,
A frantic time till Christmas Eve.
Then a hush, a quietening scene.
Now's the time to reflect and dream
On what occurred many years ago
When life was hard and very slow.
A Babe was born one mystic night,
And shepherds saw a wondrous sight.
A Saviour came to save us all
If we'll but listen to His call.
And as each Christmas passes by
I sit and ponder, 'Why? oh, why?
Are men so cruel and thoughtless too,
When if only they but knew
That they could enjoy a peace on earth
If they only remembered the Saviour's birth?'

God With Us

Oh, what Peace, as abed I lay
After the turmoil of the day!
I know that God was amid the din,
If only I could stop for Him!
No need to stop, so I am told,
My every action is like gold
If offered up to God each day –
Just as if I'd knelt to pray.
He's on the bus and in the train,
And with those people on a plane;
He sails the seas with everyone –
His constant work is never done
To serve weak folk like you and me;
He's there wherever we might be,
At work or play, in joy or sorrow;
He's here today – and still tomorrow!

Contentment

My Lord my God for you I thirst,
Listening for Your call.
I sit and wait in peace to hear
Though You may not call at all.
I try each day to contact You;
I'm sitting at Your feet.
You place Your Hand upon me
And our eyes they meet.
Your eyes they speak to me and say,
'Keep calm, my child, and rest.'
We do not always need the words;
Companionship is best.
And so I sit content in love
With peace within my soul,
And know my friend is ever there,
My target's aim and goal.

A Thought for Today

Count your blessings, not your crosses,
All your gains but not your losses.
Show some kindness to those in sorrow,
Pray for a better day tomorrow.
Show some thanks to those who give,
Try a better way to live.
Always wear a pleasant smile,
Give joy to others for a while.
When you kneel at night to pray
Thank your God for a fruitful day.

Love

Our love is Divine; not passion.
To sacrifice for those we know,
To give with one's whole devotion
All we can wherever we go.
We don't count the cost in money,
Nor expect a return to be made,
But for love of the Almighty
And eternal reward to be paid.

Easter

Enjoy your fun at Eastertide,
But remember Him who died
Upon the cross to save us all
So we might listen to the call
Of God above who sent His Son
To say, 'Live well.'
Thy Will be done.

God's Weather

I thank God for the sun,
I thank Him for the rain;
With hail, wind, snow or storm,
I thank Him still again.
Without the rain and sun
Our crops would not survive,
But after wind or snow
The sunshine will arrive,
For which I thank Him more.
I appreciate it now.
For this assorted weather
My humble head I bow.

Summer Calm

How still the sea and blue the sky.
I feel the sun's warmth as I lie
On the springy grass beneath the trees,
Yet keeping cool with gentle breeze.
I hear the water lap the shores
And see the fishermen with their oars
As from the quay they smoothly row
And way out in the bay they go.
I think back to those ages gone,
When, with Peter, James and John,
Jesus watched them cast their net
As out they sailed towards sunset.
And as I lie I wonder why
Did Jesus live, yet had to die.

Inspiration

My life is my God. From Him I cannot hide.
He is beside me always, morning, noon and eventide.
I thank Him for each day whatever it may bring.
I see the wonder of His work in everyone and thing.
As each night I lay to rest He watches over me.
Refreshed, restored, I do my best
So He'll be pleased with me.

Hallelujah!

Jesus Christ was crucified
As thunder stormed the skies.
People slunk away that day
Ashamed of wicked lies.
But came the dawn on Easter Morn,
Mankind's salvation's come!
The whole world able to rejoice:
Hallelujah! Christendom!

Me

I was born of woman, God's declaration.
He made me what I am, a body of His creation.
He gave me a wrapping of soft supple skin
With senses of hearing, sight and feelings within.
But all this is to help my soul to be seen,
Helping others their souls to redeem.
He gives me work to complete on earth;
Tasks to be done for all I'm worth.
I need God's help that I may help others –
Friends and neighbours, sisters and brothers.
I am just an apprentice serving my Lord,
And He will give me a just reward.

Crucified Jesus

My Jesus, You were crucified.
Upon the cross for us You died;
You suffered more than we shall know
At the hands of Your evil foe.

Your body it was cruelly scourged
That our evil deeds might all be purged.
Upon Your head a wreath was placed –
A crown of thorns; they You disgraced.

The soldiers mocked and spat at You
Like wild animals at a zoo;
Draped You round with a purple cloak,
They thought it was one great big joke.

You suffered all this without malice,
Even though they all were callous.
To redeem mankind from every sin
With a place in Heaven for him to win.

True Value

Richness is not wealth or money,
Riches not how much you own;
Richness is not suits or dresses,
Riches not cost of your home.

Riches are your talents well used,
Richness how you love your Lord;
Riches come from your help for others,
Richness will be your great reward.

So do not envy what others may have,
Yours will be the greater joy
If you serve your God for ever
And use your talents in his employ.

Prayer

Peoples are praying everywhere,
Every minute of the day.
And though they do all talk at once
You hear every word they say.
Some pray in adoration,
Others but for themselves.
Some pray for help for everyone,
Including those in Hell.
You never get tired of listening,
Even to those who moan for greed;
You already supply each one of them
With everything they really need.
For what one wants and what one needs
Are two very very different things.
But You make sure not what we want
But what we need, Your grace it brings.
So help me, Lord, to accept Your offer
Whatever it is You send to me,
And let me try to understand
Both Your Way and Will to see.

October

The shimmering leaves sway gently,
The wind blows through the trees;
The branches curve so gracefully,
The nests rock in the breeze.
Green foliage is turning gold
And Autumn days are nigh.
Soon now the leaves will gently float
Like feathers from the sky;
The ground will then be carpeted
With shades of every hue;
The stately trees will slowly bare
Their branches clear to view,
Awaiting now a rainy wash
And a coat of soft white snow,
Before reclothed in splendour
New growth of green will show.

Creation

Who makes the snowdrops pure and white,
And daffodils so yellow and bright.
Who makes the trees a leafy screen,
And grass that's lush and velvet green?
Who makes the birds so feathery light
So we can watch their graceful flight?
Who makes the lambs so meek and mild,
Yet frolic like a little child?
These wonders to behold we see
Are God's creations annually
To give us all serenity
And time to think of eternity.

The Storm

The steely clouds are creeping
Across the azure sky;
The nesting birds are peeping
From their vantage point on high;
The earth is still and silent
Waiting the coming storm,
The wind and rain are violent,
The air is damp and warm.
A flash of powerful lightning
Rends from sky to earth,
And to the beasts it's frightening.
But man can show his worth
Standing staunch and bold,
Although in awe of nature
O'er which he has no hold.
He has grown in stature
Praising God Almighty
For His powerful hand,
Who shows mankind how rightly
He can rule this land.

The Lord's Direction

Mid the beauty of the skies
And the wonder of the seas,
Lies the fertile crusty earth,
Full of flowers, fruit and trees.
Animals roam the fruitful land
In search of food to eat,
Fish abound in mighty oceans
Swimming, darting through the deep.
Graceful birds soar to the heavens
And nest in tallest trees,
While mankind cultivates the land
To feed his human needs.
But the soul of each of us
Is directed by the Lord
And we must nurture it each day
And live with one accord.

Awakening

There is an early morning mist
And silvery dew upon the ground.
I listen very carefully
But there's not the slightest sound.
I see the occasional early bird
Perched upon the gabled roof
And I look upon this ethereal scene
And wonder if we need more proof
To show there is a God out there
Watching and caring over this earth.
The sun advances, the view is clear.
This is the land of our earthly birth;
A land that's beautiful to behold
In every mood of the changing year.
I watch with awe and wonder why
Men destroy what we hold so dear.

Close of Day

At the end of the day
I try hard to pray
But my brain will not stay awake.
I lie in my bed,
No thoughts in my head
But I know God my spirit will take.
He will keep it at rest,
Not put it to test,
But give me a night of repose.
With the coming of dawn,
Another day's morn,
I'm refreshed from my head to my toes.
So once again
I repeat a refrain,
God be with me this day
And I'll do my best
When put to the test
To follow His word all the way.

Work

Work is life and can be joy.
Though to some it's labour and sweat.
From the moment of birth
To the last breath on earth,
It's a word we cannot forget.

We work to survive: for food to eat;
We work to be occupied.
For others we work
And we do not shirk
If we want to be satisfied.

A job well done is a noble task.
We try our level best;
And at the end of the day
We receive our pay,
And deserve our evening's rest.

When one is retired there's still work to do
The chores are always around.
We now work at leisure
Which gives us much pleasure,
For through work, joy can be found.

Spring

Like dangling pearls on plushy moss
The snowdrops hang their heads.
And crocus, purple, yellow, white,
Carpet the earthy beds.
Ingots of gold daffs stand tall
Swaying gently in the breeze;
While little birds dart to and fro
A-nesting in the trees.

Nature's New Year has begun.
The cycle we well know,
Yet every year life starts again
And sets our hearts aglow.
Creations of a craftsman
Gives us beauty to behold
And little tastes of heaven
Before our eyes unfold.

Life

O, Lord our God, how great Thou art,
As wonders of the earth we see.
For instance take the noble tree –
That bursts forth into buds galore,
It's fresh new green announcing spring;
And with its growth of fullest bloom
In summer wears a cloak of leaf
For birds to nest and fruits to bear.
Then, behold, as summer fades
Leaves mellow – rust and red and gold;
Full glory in its later life,
And carpets earth when cool winds blow.
The tree stands bare in fear and awe,
Its winter boughs covered in snow;
Do not despair, it is not dead.
It only rests to bring new life.
The cycle o'er, regenerates,
And grows in stature more than e're before.

Solitude

A garden of flowers or forest of trees,
Are both most delightful when seeking your ease.
It's tranquil and peaceful, including the sound
Of nature's own noises just floating around.
So take a deep breath of the perfumed air,
Forget all your worries but take special care
To shut out the world of commotion and noise,
Enjoy sweet contentment of natural joys.
Then back to the grindstone and labour of love,
Your mind now refreshed from the Maker above.

The Garden of the Soul

A baby's soul is virgin soil
Until the weeds have grown;
But with parental love and toil
The seeds of flowers are sown.

The rooted evil must be weeded,
Virtues allowed to bloom,
A joyous character is needed
To cheer a world of gloom.

Hope

The snow has thawed and greened the sodden grass,
The rivulets run; clear skies at last.
The birds can nest and again find food,
While waiting for Spring man's in jubilant mood.
Soon buds appear upon the bare-branched trees
And bulbs poke noses through the soil with ease.
Once more the earth emerges fresh anew
To make life good for me and you.
So Nature's cycle through each year
Shows man his life need have no fear.
From birth to death he'll grow and bloom,
Then rise again new life to resume.

Autumnal Leaves

What a glorious sight when Nature weaves
The autumn colour of the leaves.
They sparkle in the languid sun
And blow away when their day is done.
They swirl and twirl in the gusty gale
Circling in the air they sail,
Carpeting the roads and lanes,
Covering plants and soaked with rains,
Raked and gathered by gardener's hand
To be recycled for the land.
Then we wait for another year
To watch again for leaves to appear.

Sleepless Night

The night is dark and still,
The sky ablaze with stars;
No breath of wind astir.
Can I see planet Mars?
The trees are silver grey
Silhouetted 'gainst the sky.
Two chimney pots erect
Like towers standing high.
No movement on the ground.
Nature is fast asleep;
Insects and wriggly worms
Lie well below and deep.
No nightbirds can be heard;
Others are in their nests.
I stand and watch with awe;
The world appears at rest.
Then comes the rising dawn;
The sweet song of the birds.
Earth begins to waken,
And I am stuck for words.
I only sense deep feeling.
I've seen a wondrous sight.
This view I know is always there
For me to watch at night.

Autumn Vista

It's like an artist's picture
That fills my window scene.
The trees in all their glory
Stand there like a dream.
Their leaves of rust and yellow
Glisten in the golden sun
And the backing of the azure sky
Presents a view not to be outdone.
The collar'd dove sits there so still
As other birds fly round,
And a squirrel prances in and out,
Then pounces to the ground.
How city folk would love this view
If they'd find the time to look.
It's all free here to be enjoyed
Just like my picture book.

Repentance

I've fallen in the pit of sin,
Great darkness fills my soul.
A mighty war is raging in
My soul as black as coal.
My guardian angel, please help me!
Slay Satan with God's grace,
Please listen to my heartfelt plea
And lead me to the place
Where souls are cleansed and reinforced
To fight again the war.
When Satan comes I'll be endorsed
To pray to keep God's law.

My Hope

I don't want to be a demon,
Stoking coals all day
Into a fiery furnace
Without thanks or pay.
To watch the flaming fires
That never do go out.
But be allowed to go upstairs
To see what that's all about!

I don't want to be an angel,
Floating for evermore
Upon a long white fluffy cloud.
O, what an awful bore!
To play upon a harp all day
Where endless choirs sing.
I just want to be allowed
To worship Christ, our Lord and King!

Questions, Questions, Questions

Does Joseph do his carpentry,
Or Mary cook in heaven?
What food do heavenly spirits need –
Angel cake or cream from Devon?

Do the angels queue up with their harps
And clash their bowls to make the thunder?
Does Peter still catch fish and fry it
With the lightning, tearing sky asunder?

What about all the saints up there –
Do they use the clouds as tables?
And shake off all their crumbs on us
In form of snow upon our gables?

The water they spill makes raindrops
Giving drink to our poor earth –
But what do they do for clothing –
Borrow our sheets and give us mirth?

Do they sleep at night upon the stars
Beneath the silvery moon
With dreams of Jupiter and Mars,
And plan to visit them soon?

If this is life in heaven
I do not wish to go.
I'm quite content to live on earth
And make my heaven below!

A Different Story?

How would the story read
If the Tetrarch had decreed
That registration should take place
In height of summer for that race?
The towns would still as crowded be
And still no room at the inn for He
Who would be born to us that day,
But easier to bear in new mown hay.
In Bethlehem He would be born
With summer's sun to keep Him warm;
But no shepherds would attend
Nor ox nor ass required to lend
The air that stench of homelessness
That the story does confess.
There would have been no cattle stall
And no bright star to cover all.
And would the angels sing as bright
In daytime as they did at night?
He would still be born on earth, it's true,
But a different story would ensue
And not the one so full of grace
That filled that poor impoverished place.